Steps to Findi

Peace and Happiness

How to Find Peace and Happiness Within Yourself

FREE DOWNLOAD

Sign Up For My Mailing List And Get The Ultimate Inner Peace Affirmation Audio Series To Attain Nirvana and Greater Peace for FREE!

Click here to get started: www.mikemccallister.com/free

against the publisher for any reparation, damages, or monetary loss due to the information herein, either directly or indirectly.

Respective authors own all copyrights not held by the publisher.

The information herein is offered for informational purposes solely, and is universal as so. The presentation of the information is without contract or any type of guarantee assurance.

The trademarks that are used are without any consent, and the publication of the trademark is without permission or backing by the trademark owner. All trademarks and brands within this book are for clarifying purposes only and are the owned by the owners themselves, not affiliated with this document.

Introduction

The pursuit of inner peace and happiness is a goal we all share. Whether you are trying to become a millionaire or a better parent, the goal is out of a desire to become happy and content.

Haile Selassie, a Crown Prince and regent of the Ethiopian empire, once said:

> *"Peace is a day-to-day problem (and) the product of a multitude of events and judgements. Peace is not an 'is,' it is a 'becoming."*

Being peaceful is not an act of doing; it is an act of becoming that comes from within. The inner peace that we strive for is a result of a multitude of things, and as 'out-there' as this may sound, it is not impossible to accomplish that. You can be happy, satisfied, peaceful, and empowered, and can live a fulfilled and happy life.

This book aims to show you the steps you can take to experience inner peace and happiness.

Chapter 1: Understanding the Essence of Inner Peace

Inner peace is a relative term, which is why its meaning, definition, and description varies from person to person. That said, it does have an essence and foundation.

In this chapter, we shall discuss what it means to have inner peace and be in this beautiful state.

Inner Peace: An Active State of Contentment

Contrary to popular belief, inner peace is not a state of passivity or one that makes you feel dull. It is an active state of mind, one that makes you more aware, happy, and alive of yourself and your surroundings.

Inner peace is a state of being completely content, both spiritually and mentally, with considerable understanding and knowledge to keep yourself strong in times of stress and adversity. When you are at peace, you feel emotionally, psychologically, and physically healthy as well.

If you analyze your state of mind, you will realize that you tend to overthink, worry about things, and stress over issues. For instance, you probably often worry about what may happen, fret over what happened in the past, and overanalyze things you just did. When you are continually stressed, you give your mind more than it can handle, which disrupts your peace.

We call this state of jumping from one thought to another as the 'racing state of mind.' A racing state of mind keeps you from focusing on any one thing in particular. When you focus on too many things at once instead of living in the moment, you experience discontent.

How The Racing Mind Disrupts Your Quality of Life

Most of our challenges in life stem from a state of discontentment caused by a racing state of mind.

For example:

- We feel miserable because we are unaware of what we want, which is why we end up pursuing meaningless desires in life. As an example, you may think you want a fascinating, high paying career, but after achieving the goal, realize you feel emptier than you have ever felt.

- We also feel stressed when we burden ourselves with more than we can handle. In the hopes of doing everything, we fill our plates with countless activities and end up exhausting ourselves.

- Stress, frustration, and discontentment also come from not having a clear direction in life. Not knowing the direction in which our life is heading stems from not being clear about our core values and principles. When you are unaware of your guiding principles, you pursue meaningless objectives in life, which adds to your stress.

- Our life also lacks meaning and value because we dwell on the past or future. We worry about bygones long after they have happened and stress about things that may never happen. We fail to accept and understand that we live in the present moment, and it alone is what matters the most. Instead of creating memories and utilizing our present, we let it slip through our fingers and then complain of how much we are missing.

- Every issue we experience stems from a lack of clarity. Being in a wrong relationship is a lack of clarity; choosing an unfulfilling career is a lack of clarity. Investing in the wrong business, and saying hurtful things to loved ones out of spite, wasting our time in meaningless activities and the likes all stem from a lack of clarity.

- Instead of letting the past be a bygone or doing what we can do to improve the present, we overthink everything. This focus on the past does nothing but add to our burden and pressure.

Every one of these problems is easy to resolve by unlocking a state of complete inner peace. Let us now take a closer look at how inner peace changes your life for the better.

How Inner Peace Improves Life

Inner peace comes from a complete state of awareness and mindfulness that can change your life beautifully. For instance, awareness and mindfulness —as well as the inner peace and happiness they foster— can improve your life in the following ways:

- When you become aware of what you want in life, you can make better and well-informed choices that help you fulfill your genuine aspirations. Awareness makes it easier to know the kind of career you want, the type of relationships that bring you joy, and the activities in which to invest your time and energy.

- Awareness helps you stop pursuing every desire and idea that catches your fancy and enables you to go after endeavors you genuinely believe in and want to achieve. Living your life in this manner saves your time, energy, and money; it helps you invest in what matters.

- When you become mindful and aware, you stop allowing people and their wishes to affect and control you. For instance, if your father wants you to run the family business, but you want to start an organic farm, you can reject his offer in favor of your dreams.

- Awareness and mindfulness help you focus on one activity, one task, one thought, and one idea at a time, which allows you to think better and perform better at tasks. Freeing yourself from the distraction of many ideas enables you to work on one task at a time and carry it out diligently and with complete awareness. Such a level of diligence allows you to execute it well.

- The inner peace that comes from awareness and mindfulness helps you stop worrying about what went wrong or may go wrong. It enables you to make the present moment count by doing what you can do right now.

- Being aware and mindful gives you a chance to dig deeper into your thoughts, wishes, aspirations, core values, and beliefs. When you are aware of these elements, you gain a complete understanding of yourself and what you aspire for in life, which helps you find true meaning and a sense of purpose in life. When you are purposeful, you stop moving in a haywire manner. You know what you want and strive for it so that you can turn your core dreams into reality.

Unlocking and establishing true inner peace helps you clear all the unnecessary clutter from your mind. When you declutter your mind, you can declutter, organize, and cleanse other areas of your life accordingly. Decluttering different areas of your life helps you create a beautiful, meaningful, and well-rounded life that brings you pure joy, clarity, meaning, and empowerment.

The following chapters of the book will help you understand and figure out how to find pure joy and inner peace in life.

Chapter 2: Know and Embrace Who You Are

Eckhart Tolle, a German-born Canadian spiritual teacher renowned for his book *The Power of Now and A New Earth: Awakening to Your Life's Purpose* once said,

> *"You find peace not by rearranging the circumstances of your life, but by realizing who you are at the deepest level."*

Without knowing yourself, can you know what goal to pursue and what direction to steer your life? Of course not!

Unfortunately, many of us set goals and embark on journeys without this very realization, which is why we quit more goals than we accomplish, and feel internally chaotic. You can find peace, meaning, and value in life only *when you know what you truly want*. This very realization comes from knowing and embracing yourself.

Step #1: Dig deep into who you are

To find inner peace and happiness, first and foremost, you must know who you sincerely and genuinely are. If you are not aware of your most genuine needs, aspirations, beliefs, and core values, your life will lack structure and substance.

Here is what you need to do to get that clarity in life:

1. Grab a journal and pen and go somewhere peaceful.

2. Take a few deep, re-centering breaths.

3. Think of who you are and what words describe you best. These adjectives could relate to your strengths, weaknesses, qualities, and anything you think expresses who you are.

4. Make a list of your strengths and weaknesses and analyze them individually in an unbiased manner so that you are well aware of your qualities as well as your shortcomings. Undertaking this action gives you deep insight into what you want and where you wish to head in life.

5. Using those adjectives, describe yourself in a few sentences and then analyze that description objectively.

Remember that you need to do this regularly so that you keep getting clarity on who you are and where you wish to drive your life.

Step #2: Accept yourself

Knowing yourself is not sufficient to unlock your inner peace. You need to accept yourself too so that you move on with improving yourself and make peace with your faults.

When you fail to embrace yourself, you are likely to keep bashing yourself, which is likely to leave you feeling defeated, resulting in low self-esteem. When you practice self-acceptance, you stop belittling yourself, accept yourself the way you are, and strive for improvement from a healthy perspective.

To practice self-acceptance, here is what you need to do.

1. Think of all your flaws and weaknesses that hurt your self-esteem and make you feel bad about yourself.

2. Think of how these shortcomings have kept you from being happy, and if thinking about those things leaves you feeling hurt, console yourself.

3. Take a deep breath and imagine the pain and hurt exiting your system.

4. Create a positive suggestion based on acceptance. For instance, you can say, 'I love and accept myself fully and wholeheartedly' and chant it repeatedly.

5. As you practice the suggestion, close your eyes and imagine yourself feeling wholly peaceful and happy with yourself.

6. Carry out this exercise several times during the day, and you will find yourself feeling better.

When you learn to embrace everything good and bad about yourself, you stop worrying about who you are not, and instead find meaning within you. To enhance this meaning, you also need clarity of your core values.

Step #3: Find your core values and principles

Your core values, beliefs, and principles serve as the guiding forces in your life. You cannot know who you are, yearn to become, or the direction you want your life to head in until you become aware of what you believe in genuinely. Your core values are all the principles you firmly believe in and need to create a foundation for your life.

Think of the values and beliefs you strongly believe in and cannot compromise on at whatever cost. These can be related to honesty, integrity, discipline, faith, spirituality, trust, happiness, and minimalism. In case you are unclear about your core values, research and read up on different core values. You can also think about the things you genuinely believe in and have used so far to make particular decisions in life.

Write down those values and beliefs and ponder on them until they become stark. As a matter of importance, you need to spend time reflecting on your core values and ideas so that you can adopt the right beliefs. Spending time in reflection will also help you avoid wasting time on following ideals that do not conform to what you truly believe.

Is this book helping you in some way? If so, I'd love to hear about it. Your honest reviews would help readers find the right book for their needs and help me tailor the future books to yours. Reviews are the single most important factor in determining if a book succeeds, so I'm incredibly thankful for people like you who I can rely on to leave one.

Click here to leave a review for this book on any of your favorite online store:
http://www.mikemccallister.com/innerpeace

Chapter 3: Find Your Genuine Desires and Set Meaningful Goals

Once you know who you are, you need to use that knowledge to sculpt a life you truly believe in and want to live. When you implement what you believe in genuinely, you can manifest your true desires and achieve the peace you are searching for.

Eleanor Roosevelt, a renowned American diplomat, activist, and political figure once said,

"It isn't enough to talk about peace. One must believe in it. And it isn't enough to believe in it. One must work at it."

It is one thing to talk about living a peaceful life and a completely different thing to manifest that life. Manifesting the peaceful life you want requires that you figure out your genuine desires, needs, and aspirations, and then set meaningful goals centered on those desires.

Here are steps to help you

Step #4: Dig into your deepest, most genuine desires

Your genuine wants and needs can help you figure out what you truly want in life. When you are aware of your most genuine needs and desires, you can pursue what you yearn for instead of chasing whatever catches your fancy. Not knowing your deepest desire is why you have tried running five businesses in the last three years. It is also why you could not establish one of these businesses and instead quit them a few months after starting.

One of the most effective ways to uncover your most profound and most genuine needs and aspirations is to practice meditation daily. Meditation helps soothe a racing mind. It enables you to stop overthinking stuff, jumping from one branch of thought to another, and instead focus on one thing at a time.

Meditation is a useful tool that helps you cultivate mindfulness. Mindfulness is a state of complete, nonjudgmental, and accepting awareness. When you meditate and become mindful, you stay in the here and now, and without worrying about what happened or may happen, you peacefully exist.

We have many meditative techniques, but a simple and highly effective one is mindfulness breathing meditation. Mindfulness breathing calms you, gives you a break from stressful thoughts, and gradually helps you uncover and understand your most authentic feelings, beliefs, and aspirations.

Here is how you can practice it:

1. Sit comfortably and peacefully in a quiet room.

2. Take deep breaths to assuage your stress and close your eyes.

3. Gently, bring your awareness to your breath and inhale through your nose.

4. As you inhale, watch your in-breath and stay one with it. Remaining connected to your breath means you must focus on it alone.

5. Exhale from your mouth and calmly watch your out-breath too.

6. Keep breathing in this very manner for 2 to 5 minutes.

7. You may wander off in thought several times during your practice. Every time you notice this, calmly bring your

attention back to your breath and continue observing it peacefully. You may need to do this several times so that you can stay focused on your breathing. That's okay because if you are new to meditation, you will struggle with being focused, which is why you need to be patient with yourself. Being patient helps you feel peaceful when in chaotic situations. It trains you to divert your attention from the distractions around you and focus on what matters.

8. Once you feel calmer, which could be in that session or after a few sessions, think of what you yearn for the most in life. Think of any area of your life you wish to improve the most and then reflect on what you desire to achieve in that area. If your health matters the most to you, think of what you want to accomplish in this area.

9. Similarly, think of different areas of your life and pick out the most important ones. With every area, think of what you would like to accomplish. Reflect on your relationships, career, love life, health, wealth, abundance, spirituality, and other aspects of your life you consider paramount to your wellbeing.

10. While figuring out what you want, ensure to do so in light of your core values and beliefs. When what you want aligns with your core principles, you start living a harmonious, well-balanced life.

11. Ask yourself questions like: 'What do I want in life?' 'What brings me pure joy?' 'What gives me meaning?' Asking yourself these and similar questions helps you gain clarity of your hidden desires.

Doing this once or twice isn't enough: you need to have regular introspection sessions started by mindfulness breathing meditation. Write down the answers to your questions and all your findings so you can keep a record of them. Once you have this list of answers, go through it repeatedly to make better sense of things and establish a nexus among your findings.

Step #5: Find your vision and mission in life

Based on the areas you wish to improve in life and your core values, figure out your vision in life. Your life's vision is the broader scope you have for your life; we call it *the direction in which you wish to steer your life.*

For instance, if you wish to be healthy and to encourage others to live a healthy life, your vision could be to become physically and mentally fit and to share that knowledge.

You must have a vision for life because when you have one, the direction in which your life is heading becomes more evident, which is very important. If you set goals without having a clear vision, you are likely to feel meaningless and confused after achieving your goals. You would not get a sense of completion. Hence, it is crucial to know your vision in life so that you have a sense of purpose that helps unlock your inner peace.

Once you have clarity on your vision, use it to find a mission you can use as your long-term goal. That mission is a means to achieve your vision, and once you accomplish that, you can have another purpose. Having a mission is crucial because it allows you to move closer to your vision. Keeping in mind your vision, set a mission, and then embark on the journey of achieving it.

Step #6: Set and achieve goals

Peace and joy come from a sense of accomplishment and fulfillment. When you see yourself achieving meaningful goals, you feel good about yourself, which helps unlock a state of profound peace and contentment.

With your vision and mission in mind, set meaningful goals, and create plans to fulfill them. Here is how to do that:

- With the timeline of your mission in mind, divide it into different milestones spread over 3 to 6 months.

- Every milestone needs to have smaller weekly targets, and every weekly target needs to have daily goals.

- Make sure that every goal you achieve aligns with the values you believe in and relates to your vision. Do not spend your time and energy setting and achieving meaningless goals. That will only drain you and make it difficult to live peacefully.

- Plan how to achieve every daily and weekly target so you have daily and weekly To-do lists to work regularly.

- Once you have a detailed plan, go through every step of the process, analyze tasks, and then start working on them one by one.

- There needs to be something meaningful to look forward to every day, week, and month. When such is the case, you will keep achieving one milestone after another and moving towards your end goal in a streamlined approach.

Once you achieve meaningful goals, you will feel good about yourself. To ensure you invest your emotions, time, energy, and money in tasks that unlock your inner peace and happiness, use the next set of strategies.

Step #7: Acknowledge Your Mistakes and Flaws (Avoid Perfectionism)

It's healthy to strive for excellence, but insisting on perfection is an uphill battle that will always work against you. Always pursuing perfectionism will make you never feel good enough about yourself.

So as you strive to improve yourself each day, accept that you are going to make mistakes and fail, and make a constant effort to acknowledge your weaknesses and flaws.

But what if you're an "obstinate" perfectionist?

However, if you really consider yourself a perfectionist- in the strict sense of the word- it also helps to look at the worst-case scenario, and how likely or unlikely it is to occur just as it does in realizing that there is probably something that you can do in that isolated situation.

If you have to, list out all the worst things that could happen and compare them to the most likely scenario, and then talk them through with someone you trust. You'll realize that this simple step does help get those dark thoughts out of your mind.

Chapter 4: Go On a Decluttering Spree

Peace comes from focusing on what matters to you and from not overwhelming yourself with more than you can handle. When you do things, you feel good about and surround yourself with activities, people, and an uplifting environment instead of one that pulls you down, you feel joyous and peaceful.

To ensure that you achieve this state, declutter every aspect of your life and free it from things and elements that pollute it in any way. Decluttering and organizing your life helps eliminate what is meaningless so that what remains are things that enrich and make your life worthwhile.

Here is what you need to do to declutter and unleash your inner peace.

Step #6: Declutter your home

Start decluttering your home from everything that makes it chaotic and deprives it of the warmth, peace, and comfort you look for in your haven. If all you see is clutter, junk, and meaningless stuff everywhere you look in your house, you will feel disturbed.

If every nook and corner of your bedroom has documents, broken furniture, clothes, and the likes, you will never feel comfortable. You will feel chaotic every time you enter this space, which will eat away at your peace.

Infuse peace and meaning into your home by decluttering and eliminating everything that clutters and destroys its true essence. Start with decluttering any one room in your house and move on to others once you fully declutter that one room. You can also work on more than one room at a time by decluttering one corner every day.

Eliminate items you have spares of, old and worn out stuff, things you haven't used in ages and anything else that does not bring you comfort, joy, meaning, or value. If you have an old bean bag covered in dust because you don't use it, get rid of it. If your kitchen cabinets have mugs you haven't used in 2 years, donate or discard them. Toss out useless and worn-out things so that you can create space for meaningful things. Your house and mind will instantly feel spacious and peaceful.

Step #7: Get rid of toxic people from your life

As you have decluttered to improve the environment of your house, create a comfortable environment by surrounding yourself with positive, inspirational, and like-minded people who support and love you.

Jim Rohn, a well-known self-help author, and motivational speaker, once said:

'You are the average of the five people you spend the most time with.'

This quote holds immense truth because if you analyze yourself, you will realize that you are the total of the ideologies of the people with whom you spend most of your time. If you usually feel chaotic, confused, and stressed, you probably spend a large portion of your time in the company of negative influences whose toxicity rubs off on you.

To cultivate happiness and inner calm, surround yourself with people who epitomize these character traits. Analyze the influence of different people in your social circle and observe how they affect you. If they weigh you down, and add to your stress, it is best to distance yourself from them and gradually replace them with positive influences.

Step #8: Spend time doing meaningful activities only

As you adopt the habit of spending time with positive people, also embrace the habit of spending your time doing positive, meaningful activities. If being in a debating club, swimming club, playing golf, and going out clubbing, is exhausting, filter out the ones you do not wish to engage in anymore.

Stick to activities you enjoy and that relate to your goals, principles, values, and things that bring you absolute joy. Get rid of everything else that weighs you down and things you engage in to please others. Once in a blue moon, it is fine to do something for the sake of someone's happiness but doing that all the time will disrupt your peace.

Create a list of activities you enjoy and ensure to spend time doing them —at least 3 to 5 times during the week. Create weekly rituals based on these activities so that you engage in something pleasurable frequently. Every Tuesdays could be 'baking' days, Thursdays could be 'movie night out with friends,' and Sundays could be 'spa days.' You get the idea.

Step #9: Cleanse your mind of polluting ideas

Your mind houses all your thoughts. If toxic thoughts pollute this sacred space, you will feel miserable, unhappy, and depressed. Your self-esteem, confidence, and emotional stability depends on the thoughts and ideas in your head.

Spend some time analyzing your thoughts, beliefs, and ideas, and filter out those that have an ounce of negativity. If you believe your potential can never increase or that you don't deserve to be successful, then you have limiting beliefs that hold you back. Understand that you possess incredible power that can only improve if you keep trying.

Similarly, observe and analyze other beliefs and ideas you nurture and then filter out from your mind the unnecessary, meaningless, and negative ones. Replace them with positive, uplifting, and healthier ones that help you think optimistically. Optimism helps you feel emotionally and psychologically at peace, which improves your quality of life.

As you work on this, make every moment count and work to infuse every moment of your life with peace, clarity, and joy. The next chapter talks about how you can do this.

Chapter 5: Make Moments Count

Every moment you spend worrying about what you don't have or what-could-have-been leads to increased pressure and worry. Peace and joy come from within you. Only when you live every moment to its fullest without any judgment can you unlock that state of wellbeing.

Here are a few ways to ascertain the accomplishment of this endeavor.

Step #10: Nurture gratitude

Gratitude makes life sweeter, more meaningful, and content. The minute you shift your attention from what you don't have to the many blessings in your life, you feel hopeful, positive, and naturally peaceful.

Start every day by thanking the universe —or any power you believe in— for two or more of your blessings. That could be having clean clothes to wear or waking up to kisses from your partner. When you sit down for your breakfast, thank the universe for putting food on your table. When completing a project on your computer, give thanks for the opportunity. When you go to the bathroom to shower, be thankful for having enough clean water with which to shower. Whatever you do, be grateful for it.

Ensure that you do this very consciously so that you embrace the blessing present in your life right now and feel truly grateful for it. When the day ends, you will feel happier and positive for your many blessings —you will be brimming with joy. Do this daily to build a habit of it and to keep feeling peaceful with each passing day.

Step #11: Live in and seize the moment

Living in the moment is crucial to making the most of it. To live in and capture the moment, whatever task you are doing, do it slowly and with increased attention. Visualize yourself doing it successfully, and before starting it, tell yourself how good a job you will do. Engage your senses in the experience by focusing on how the task makes you feel, the sounds you hear, etc.

When you do this, you become more involved in the mission, which improves your productivity and helps you live in the moment.

Additionally, whatever emotions you feel in a moment, embrace them acceptingly without judging them. Stop labeling yourself, your feelings, and the people around you. Being angry isn't bad; neither is it wrong to feel jealous. When you accept emotions and a person for what and who he/she is, you stop associating unnecessary meaning to it, which cultivates inner peace and happiness.

Step #12: Be accountable

Instead of looking for people to blame for your mistakes, failures, and poor decisions, take accountability for your actions and decisions. If you followed the wrong advice, that's on you because you had a choice. If you opted for an unhealthy relationship, you need to act responsibly for it because the universe did not push you into it.

Taking accountability for your actions helps you become more responsible and mature. It curtails the tendency to complain and helps you focus on being better. Moreover, it helps you understand that you are in charge of your life and that if you wish to be happy, you need to make better choices.

Step #13: Be positive

If you perceive every experience from a negative lens, you will feel terrible internally because nothing will bring you joy.

You need to improve your perception of things by thinking and acting positively.

Even when in worst-case scenarios, try to find the good. Think of every experience as a learning experience and focus on what you can improve. The more you do this, the more you will find plenty to be happy about and to be grateful for. In essence, gratefulness is one of the critical steps to inner peace and happiness.

Focusing on what you can learn helps you build a can-do and positive attitude that keeps you from crying over spilled milk and instead look for actionable solutions. When you become solution-focused, it becomes easier to achieve your goals, which helps you feel better.

Step #14: Live for yourself

Living for yourself is paramount to being happy and peaceful. To start living for yourself, ensure that whatever you do brings you happiness. Start by not comparing yourself with others and by not trying to control things beyond your reach. Focus on improving yourself and loving yourself the way you are even as you work on self-improvement.

Additionally, do things that bring you joy even if sometimes, that means doing nothing at all. When you live for yourself, you feel empowered and in control, which makes your life more enjoyable.

Step #15: Spread kindness and happiness

Self-actualization is a basic human need. It comes from spreading joy, kind-heartedness, and positivity. Just as you take care of yourself, do so for others out of the pure reason of feeling good about yourself. Doing this helps you take responsibility for being kind and compassionate to others and for caring for them.

Help out loved ones, be kind to strangers, and spend time doing community work at shelter homes, orphanages, and charitable organizations. Being involved helps you get closer to humanity and unlocks your empathetic side. The more empathetic you are, the more content you feel. This leads me to the next point below:

Step #16: Forgive

According to **Gerald Jampolsky**, *"Inner peace can be reached only when we practice forgiveness. Forgiveness is letting go of the past, and is therefore the means for*

correcting our misperceptions."
It's a lot easier to find inner peace when your heart is not tied to a negative feeling from a past event. Forgiveness is essential since you're always linked to a person you're not willing to forgive. Your thoughts will always tend to go back to that person who wronged you and the things they did over and over again. No matter what you do, you can never achieve true peace like this because this would result in inner turmoil from time to time.

You need to understand four things before you take action:

1. When you forgive, you don't just release the person but set yourself free from that agony as well.

2. Forgiveness doesn't necessarily mean you're excusing the person's actions.

3. Forgiveness doesn't mean you have to tell them that they're forgiven

4. Forgiveness doesn't mean you have to block yourself from having any more feelings about that situation.

So acknowledge and accept the growth you experienced because of what happened. What did you learn about yourself from it, or about your boundaries and needs?

Next, think about the person who wronged you. When they hurt you, this person was trying to have some need met. What do you think this need really was, and why did they go about it in a hurtful way?

Lastly, say the words to yourself, "I forgive myself" and explain why you are doing so.

By forgiving others, you forgive yourself as well- for accepting to hurt yourself with the held resentment and pain for so long.

If you dedicatedly work on these steps, your heart will soon start brimming with joy and peace.

Conclusion

You are amazing; it is about time you realized that. Harness that power and use it to build a peaceful life.

This book has equipped you with every strategy you need to achieve this goal. Now take action!

Is this book helping you in some way? If so, I'd love to hear about it. Your honest reviews would help readers find the right book for their needs and help me tailor the future books to yours. Reviews are the single most important factor in determining if a book succeeds, so I'm incredibly thankful for people like you who I can rely on to leave one.

Click here to leave a review for this book on any of your favorite online store:
http://www.mikemccallister.com/innerpeace

FREE DOWNLOAD

Sign Up For My Mailing List And Get The Ultimate Inner Peace Affirmation Audio Series To Attain Nirvana and Greater Peace for FREE!

Click here to get started: www.mikemccallister.com/free

Author's Note

Thank you again for downloading this book!

Writing and speaking about the importance of inner peace and mental wellbeing has been closest to my heart, ever since 2017, when I lost my father. So much so, if there could be a point in time to see a sudden change in me, that would be it. Living in different continents and trying to get home in time as fast as a plane could go did not help. Unfortunately, I did not make it in time. I could not say my final good-bye. And I could not have all the conversations I thought of coming back to later.

The death of my father triggered a series of events in my personal life which not only affected my personal and professional relationships but shook me to the core leading to anxiety and panic attacks. As a result, my corporate poster boy rank was soon taken away and I was left to be a nobody which took its toll further.

Getting back was not easy. It took months of counselling, meditation and mindfulness to make peace with myself and others. But it was worth it. Along this journey my outlook on life changed. I realized that material pleasures are important but inner peace and mental wellbeing is priceless. And so, I began writing this series to help others chase the right things in life.

For blogs and podcasts visit

http://www.mikemccallister.com/

Also By Mike McCallister

Click here for my body of work:
www.mikemccallister.com/books

- Steps to Finding Inner Peace and Happiness - How to Find Peace and Happiness Within Yourself (Buddha on the Inside Book 1)

- How To Meditate: Learn How To Meditate Step By Step And Reap The Benefits Of Meditation Everyday + Tips On How To Meditate Better (Buddha on the Inside Book 2)

- How To Be Mindful Of Thoughts: Steps To Achieving Mindfulness And Living In The Moment (Buddha on the Inside Book 3)

- Emotional Mastery Blueprint: How to Control Your Emotions To Improve Your Social Skills And Master Your Thoughts And Emotions (Buddha on the Inside Book 4)

- A-Z Guide On How To Start Being Positive: The A-Z Of How To Think Positive And Be Happy

Thank you, and good luck!

Preview Of 'How To Meditate: Learn How To Meditate Step By Step And Reap The Benefits Of Meditation Everyday + Tips On How To Meditate Better (Buddha on the Inside Book 2)'

At times, especially when it seems like obstacles are the only thing around us, life can become so challenging that focusing on your goals and moving forward with clarity becomes a struggle.

In such moments, you ought to have at your disposal tools and strategies that can help make every process, journey, and endeavor meaningful and enjoyable for you. **Meditation** is one such tool. It primarily focuses on improving your sense of purpose, wisdom, clarity, focus, peace, and meaning in life.

Ajahn Brahm, a renowned British-Australian Theravada Buddhist monk, once said,

"Meditation is like a gym in which you develop the powerful mental muscles of calm and insight."

Meditation helps exercise your mind so that it becomes powerful and robust while maintaining its flexibility. By unlocking and harnessing its true potential, you can achieve all your goals.

In the pages that follow, you will learn everything you need to learn about meditation, including actionable tips and meditative techniques you can use to make meditation a constant in your everyday life. Every passage you read and page you turn will breed in you the interest and motivation needed to make meditation a routine practice.

Start reading the guide today so that you can learn how to use meditation to unlock and embrace a truly remarkable life.

Click here to check out the rest of 'How To Meditate: Learn How To Meditate Step By Step And Reap The Benefits Of Meditation Everyday + Tips On How To Meditate Better (Buddha on the Inside Book 2)':
http://www.mikemccallister.com/meditation

Printed in Great Britain
by Amazon

42701382R00030